Genesis 3:15; 49:10;
Matthew 1; 4:1–11; 10:1–4; 26–28;
Luke 2; Hebrews 11 for children

Written by Martha Streufert Jander
Illustrated by Chris Wold Dyrud

CONCORDIA PUBLISHING HOUSE · SAINT LOUIS

It was at the very beginning of time
When the world was all fresh and tame
That the first people sinned,
Though God was their Friend,
And things were never the same.

It was Adam and Eve who sinned in that place.
“It won’t matter,” the devil had cried.
So they thought they might be,
As they ate of that tree,
Just like God. But the snake had lied.

God talked a long while to Adam and Eve.
He asked them, "Just what have you done?"
Then He promised the glorious,
Mighty, victorious
Gift of His only Son.

The Gift did not come for a very long time,
Not even for thousands of years.
God's people waited long,
Now and then with a song,
But sometimes they cried bitter tears.

God promised the Gift to Noah and his sons,
To Abraham, Isaac, and Jacob as well.
To Judah, to Obed,
The kings and the nomads—
The Prophets His coming did tell.

After many long years, God sent down the Gift—
A Babe born in Bethlehem's night.
And Mary, His mother,
And Joseph, His father,
Knew this Child would set all things right.

The Gift who was Jesus, the most holy Child,
Grew up strong in spirit and in heart.
He obeyed all the time;
He always would mind.
Jesus grew wise in every part.

The Gift who was Jesus grew up tall and strong.
He saw the Father's work He could do.
He stood up to temptation,
Never gave in to Satan.
He was ready for all He would do.

Jesus chose twelve men to be His disciples.
He preached the Good News of God's love.
He healed all the sick ones;
He strengthened the weak ones.
He told them of heaven above.

The Gift who was Jesus kept giving and giving.
He lived by His Father's good will.
He loved, He obeyed,
He taught, and He prayed.
Yet more work awaited Him still.

Jesus wept as He prayed to His Father in heaven,
"Not My will but Yours be done."
Then Jesus died on the cross.
He suffered our loss—
And the vict'ry over sin was won.

But the Gift's best surprise would happen on Sunday,
The third day after He died.
Jesus rose from the grave.
It's the world that He saved.
He's not dead; He's alive! He's alive!

The Gift that is Jesus is still ours forever—
His gladness, His love, and His grace.
Our sins are forgiven;
He's promised us heaven.
We'll sing praises to Him in that place.

Dear Parent,

Jesus is alive! He lives and reigns with the Father and the Holy Spirit in heaven. What a gift! What a surprise! He's the Gift the Father gave to us—to you and to your children—and to your children's children. "But the steadfast love of the LORD is from everlasting to everlasting on those who fear Him, and His righteousness to children's children" (Psalm 103:17).

God wants you and your children to know how much He loves you, that He forgives all your sins and waits for you in heaven. This forgiveness did not come cheaply or easily. It did not come with an indulgent smile and a pat on the head. Indeed, being God, He could not say, "Well, we know you did wrong, but we'll just forget about it, shall we? Just be careful next time."

No, God's holiness, His justice, demanded payment for the sin of all humankind. Death, eternal death, should have come to Adam and Eve. But God chose instead for His Son to be sacrificed in their—and our—place. Jesus had to suffer and die, to give up His life so we might live.

Oh, celebrate that new life with your child! Let him or her know how much God loved through the death of His Son. With your family, tell others that Good News too!

Rejoice together in Jesus' glorious resurrection from the dead and the assurance that He has, without any doubt, conquered death and sin and hell and Satan and made heaven a sure place for us!

The Author